SCHOLASTIC Phonics

Athletics

Published in the UK by Scholastic Education, 2023

Scholastic Distribution Centre, Bosworth Avenue, Tournament Fields, Warwick, CV34 6UQ

Scholastic Ireland, 89E Lagan Road, Dublin Industrial Estate, Glasnevin, Dublin, D11 HP5F

SCHOLASTIC and associated logos are trademarks and/or registered trademarks of Scholastic Inc.

www.scholastic.co.uk

© 2023 Scholastic

1 2 3 4 5 6 7 8 9   3 4 5 6 7 8 9 0 1 2

Printed by Ashford Colour Press

The book is made of materials from well-managed, FSC®-certified forests and other controlled sources.

A CIP catalogue record for this book is available from the British Library.
ISBN 978-0702-32104-7

All rights reserved. This book is sold subject to the condition that it shall not, by way of trade or otherwise, be lent, hired out or otherwise circulated in any form of binding or cover other than that in which it is published. No part of this publication may be reproduced, stored in a retrieval system, or transmitted in any form or by any other means (electronic, mechanical, photocopying, recording or otherwise) without prior written permission of Scholastic.

Every effort has been made to trace copyright holders for the works reproduced in this publication, and the publishers apologise for any inadvertent omissions.

Author
Rachel Russ

Editorial team
Rachel Morgan, Vicki Yates, Alison Gilbert, Jennie Clifford

Design team
Dipa Mistry, Andrea Lewis, We Are Grace

Photographs
Cover Franz Metelec/Shutterstock
p4 santypan/iStock
p1, 5, 22–23 kupicoo/iStock
p5, 14, 24 Wavebreakmedia/iStock
p6–7, 24 PeopleImages/iStock
p8–9 ZamoraA/iStock
p10, 11 oleg66/iStock
p12, 15 Real Sports Photos/Shutterstock
p13, 24 Soonthorn Wongsaita/Shutterstock
p16, 20–21 technotr/iStock
p3, 17 Brenda Carson/Shutterstock
p18 South_agency/iStock
p19 Papa Annur/Shutterstock

Help your child to read!

This book practises these letters and letter sounds.
Point and say the sounds with your child:

ay (as in 'way')   ou (as in 'sound')   ea (as in 'leap')

Your child may need help to read these common tricky words:

of   they   to   push   the
when   she   put   like   go

Before reading
- Look at the cover picture and read the title together. Read the back cover blurb to your child.
- Ask your child: *Have you ever taken part in a race? What happened?*
- Talk about the image in the magnifying glass.

During reading
- If your child gets stuck on a word, remind them to sound it out and then blend the sounds to read the word: s-ou-n-d, sound.
- If they are still stuck, show them how to read the word.
- Enjoy looking at the pictures together. Pause to talk about the information.

After reading
- Talk about the images on page 24. What can your child tell you about them?
- Ask your child: *What do athletes need to do to improve?*
- Discuss which event your child liked the best.

Athletics is a sport with a mix of...

...running,

…jumping

…and tossing!

Athletics tests human speed, skill and strength.

Running
Sprinters run a short way.

They need power to push off from the blocks when they hear the start sound. Speed helps them finish first.

Marathon runners run a long way.

They attempt to continue running without stopping.

Jumping

In the long jump, contestants jump a long way. Power and speed helps them run up.

Then they leap, leaning to reach as far as they can.

In the high jump, contestants must leap higher than the bar.

They run up to the bar and then jump.

This contestant arches her back as she tries to get across the bar.

Tossing

In shot-put, the shot is held with a firm grip.

shot

Contestants must turn and toss the shot a long way.

The javelin is like a long spear.

The javelin is held with the arm reaching up high.

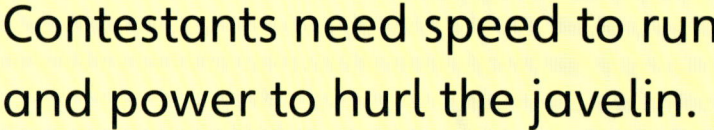
Contestants need speed to run and power to hurl the javelin.

The javelin sticks in the ground.

In the hammer, contestants turn around, swinging the hammer.

the hammer

They let the hammer go and it flies across the ground.

To reach the top at athletics, contestants need strength, power and speed.

This means training hard.

Talk about it!